So You Want to be a…Landlord?

Written by

T. Renee

This book is a work of non-fiction. Names and places have been changed to protect the privacy of all individuals. The events and situations are true.

ISBN: 1-4107-9414-8 (e-book)
ISBN: 1-4107-9413-X (Paperback)

This book is printed on acid free paper.

1stBooks - rev. 11/07/03

Acknowledgements

Giving Honor to God who is the head of my Life. To my wonderful Soul Partner, husband and friend, (all in one) James Harris, Sr. To my kids, James Jr., Trenell, and Jenese, always have a plan and stick to it. To my father, Marvin Edwards, Sr., mother, Alrita Edwards. To my family and friends, God is the answer. To my Spiritual Guides: Rev. James and Patsy Brown, Bishop Wayne T. and Pastor Beverly Jackson. A special Thank you to Ms. Martha Jean "The Queen" Steinberg who has gone to be with the Lord, for being on the radio when I needed to hear the Positive sides of Reality! To my wonderful neighbors on that "Fire" street, Cheryl and Ron, Loretta and Eleanor, Paul and Joe.

Last but not least, to the many families who were the best tenants a Landlord could want. Thank You for making my job easy and blessed!

In Loving Memory:

Rosalie "Ga Ga" Edwards♥

John "Uncle Frank" Edwards♥

Lou "Granny" Travis♥

Emma Lou "mom" Edwards♥

Cheryl Travis-Taylor♥

Daniel "Granddad" Travis♥

Charles "Charlie" Haddad♥

In The Beginning

This book is a guide to prepare you of what to expect and detailing a few circumstances of being a Landlord. Your job being a Landlord requires patience, keen perception, fix-it skills and the ability to say NO in the times of a tenants' personal crisis. (I know that sounds cruel but you'll read what I mean) You must be able to keep calm when your rent is not paid on time. You should have a very detailed lease. (Late charges, fees, pet charges) Read it more than twice to make sure everything you need in writing is established, in case of "legal inconveniences". There will be a time where Biblical phrases arise in your mind, for example, "God help, Patience of Job, Peace be still". There will be some tense moments depending on the situation. Everyone's personality is not the same.

Being a Landlord is not always about the "Benjamin's". My husband and I renovated and rented homes for many years and it was a rewarding experience. Good Luck!

Table of Contents

Acknowledgements...iii

In The Beginning.. v

Story 1 1

Story 2 9

Story 3 16

Story 4 23

Story 5 30

Story 6 35

Story 7 40

Story 8 45

Story 9 54

My Personal Opinion 64

About the Author... 66

Story 1

1978, we're leaving Chicago, couldn't seem to get above anything let alone water. The cost of living was just too high and we always wanted to buy our own home. Here we are on I-94 east to Detroit. The American dream was to work at one of the "Big Fours". Good pay, benefits and a full night's sleep at 2 a.m. That's when the bars closed in comparison to Chicago where we would stay out all night without getting a chance to clear our head from hangovers. Mother lived there so we stayed with her for almost a month until we found a place of our own. All of my sisters (3) brothers (7) were still at home, yes, it was kind of crowded. The house we went to look at was for sale on a Land Contract. I didn't know what it was but I would find out. I couldn't believe it. The mortgage note was "ninety dollars" a month. Well without a job, ninety dollars wasn't much to have a roof over your head and eventually be the owner. The sellers were moving to the suburbs and didn't need two mortgages. The house had belonged to their grandparents before they had moved in five years earlier. We didn't need any furniture but they were leaving everything in this house.

They had bought all new everything for the new one. What a yard sale I'm going to have! There were plenty of yard sales in Michigan. Families would have them in garages, on porches, even in the persons' own house. I rarely saw these kind of sales in Chicago. There was a dining room set consisting of the table and buffet. This table was gorgeous. It had the original fold-up covering on top and underneath was beautiful oak wood. The buffet was likewise, without a scratch on it. Were these people nuts or what? In the kitchen was an old Sears stove with an extra oven broiler with storage for pots, a clock on top with a light and there was even a light inside the oven. Oh, I forgot and also a griddle in the middle in addition to the four burners.

The placed looked as if it had not painted any of the five years they were there. It's a good thing Babe (that's what I called my hubby) knew how to do interior and exterior decorating, because this place really needed some help. On to the upstairs, where we noticed someone was a cheapskate. The paneling was turned with going east and west instead of north and south. You know, the brown paneling with the black lines on it. It's the cheapest in the store. Looking around I wondered, where are the electrical outlets? The room is about 12x24 and I only see one. Cheap, cheap, cheap. In the other room, mind you this is a finished attic, it's about the same size with the same paneling. Electrical sockets? One. Good thing we know an electrician.

We've signed the paperwork, gotten the keys and off they go to their new paradise. Two weeks later, Mr. Reinhart told us that they have been flooded, the furniture didn't arrive on time and the appliances were late. Looking over this investment, it's going to be time consuming. The living room and dining room took three coats of paint and I swept the dust off first. New tile was put on the kitchen floor, which made me real happy since I was the designated cook and the walls took only one coat of paint. I picked Kelly Green. It was a cross between the color of money and grass. Most of the beds and living room furniture was tossed out or sold. We had nice hardwood floors but when we can afford it, I want carpet! There was no front porch, just four steps. Babe has lots of time on his hands until he finds employment, so he would start working on repairs. Our six year old loved the fact that she has her own room now. The closets were just big enough for a six year olds wardrobe. Very tiny. I don't know where Babe is going to hang his things because our closet was the same size "tiny" and I needed a lot of room for my things. Maybe he'll make a big one upstairs.

On the street where we lived, there were three generations of family. Some of the neighbors came down to introduce themselves since they knew the sellers. The block was culturally mixed and everyone seemed to get along fine with each other. There were a few families with small children that went to the same school as my daughter Marie. She was thrilled to have someone to play with her age and some of the kids were in her class. Babe has gone to all four car plants and put in applications and every one of them say the same thing.

"We're not hiring at this time." He also applied at a meat processing plant down the street from the house. There was no extra income coming in besides our unemployment from Illinois, so we went to the local Department of Social Services office to get some kind of assistance. The place was crowded and kids were crying and restless. The parents seemed aggravated and tired of waiting to see a Social Worker. We waited four hours before someone called our name. She gave us an appointment to come back but we were able to get food stamps the same day. The application wanted your whole life history. It was twenty-five pages long. The food stamps came in handy because we needed some food in our "spacious" refrigerator. God was certainly in the picture to bless us with this place without a job. If we had to sell newspapers, we were going to get the ninety dollars. The house was coming along and we had lots of decorating work to keep us busy for a long time. The meat company hadn't called and our appointment at the DSS office was soon. No one called from the car plants. A neighbor had suggested that Babe go to the MESC (Michigan

Employment Security Commission) because applications were sometimes available for truck driving jobs. He already had a chauffeur's license. The worker approved our case and we would be getting some money in two weeks, just in time for our house note to be paid. (whew)

Standing in front of our first house, 1978

Story 2

Surprise, three months later we got a call from the meat company. They wanted Babe to start in a week to drive one of the trucks and starting pay was $8.00 an hour. With many stores opening up in the city, the company had lots of delivery stops. A lot of drivers were getting robbed and that made me very nervous about him being on the street after dark. There were lots of robberies. He never got robbed, probably because he spoke to anyone hanging around the store. He would have a look on his face that would let you know he wasn't taking any shit. The other drivers would complain about the way the Chaldean store owners would talk to them, or want them to practically put the meats in the freezer when they were only suppose to drop the meat off at the rear of the store. This job lasted a year. Mental stress along with late hours would take over and he couldn't handle it anymore.

We went to a flea market to look for things for the house and noticed lots of construction sites. He stopped to fill out an application for a laborer position. In addition to home improvements, he could build with his hands. (Lucky me) He was hired and I had time now to work in the house alone. I continued to redecorate the house with the paint supplies we had left over. I had lots of ideas for Marie's room and since there were two bedrooms upstairs, one of them could be her very own playroom. I pulled the entire paneling down (that was put up wrong), and put drywall up and painted over it. The room looks so much brighter. I was kind of good at this to my surprise. Our electrician friend put in the long awaited electrical sockets. When winter came, construction was slow and the company started laying off people. Babe went to the unemployment office again to apply for some funds. ADC was out. We had just gotten off and it was too much hassle.

The social workers acted like they were paying us out of their slush fund, and their attitude was the pits. We probably Could get food stamps again depending on the amount of the unemployment check.

There was a HUD house across the street from us boarded up and we thought about buying it to rent out for extra income. Babe went down to the real estate office and they wanted him to fill out paperwork and submit a bid. The real estate agent gave us a tour of the place and it had lots of potential. Lots of work had to be done to it before anyone could live in here. A deposit was required to bid. Where would we get three hundred dollars? We resumed getting food stamps since we were eligible with the unemployment coming in. This week we'll save one hundred and fifty dollars and ask Mother if we could get a loan for the rest. She said yes and we took our sealed bid to the HUD office. The bids would be open a week later. While waiting we did some more work on our own house. The gutters needed to be cleaned and all of the projects inside were just about completed. It took a whole year!

Today's the day. The bids were open and we won. What a surprise! Now to come up with twenty-seven hundred dollars. We had some money put aside and maybe we would sell the

Monte Carlo. It was in good shape but could we get three grand for it? That car sure brought us through that snowstorm in '78. We could use the extra three hundred for supplies to get it ready for renting. The construction company hadn't called Babe back yet, so he had the extra time to work on the rental if we closed the deal. We tried to get another loan from Mother but she didn't have it. We had already paid back the first loan and she wished she could help us again. There was no one else to ask so we started praying more than ever. I sure didn't want to lose that deposit money. There were only two days before the deadline.

Babe was taking an afternoon nap. When he woke up, he said he had a dream about a rabbit. "It was so vivid, so real". Well, we didn't know what dreaming about a rabbit meant so we thought about playing a number in the lottery. I called Mother and she had one of those dream books. The book had a three-digit number per word or name for whatever you wanted to look up. Some of those books have two sets of three digits plus four digit numbers to boot. I was glad she didn't have that one. Rabbit was 189. Since we needed three grand, he put six dollars on the number straight. You could win five hundred dollars per dollar you played. I wanted him to box the number because anyway it came, he would be able to get some money. He said, "I want it straight!" He always was a mean gambler. The drawing came on at seven-thirty. The balls would jump up through three different tubes. The first ball, ONE. The second ball, EIGHT. What! I was excited. The third ball, NINE! I'm dreaming right? He was outdone, "Oh my God". I was too. Now we can get the house!! What luck. No more uncertain jobs. No one looking down your throat or bossing you around like the meat place. This could be the beginning of something. Self-employment. I like those words. We could charge up to three hundred fifty a month for rent. That wouldn't be too much in 1980, especially for a whole house. In Chicago, houses rented for five hundred and up. Time to go to the real estate office. Mr. Sid, the realtor, would be surprised to see we're ready to close the deal and pick up our keys!

"So you want to be a landlord", he asked? Babe told him he can't find steady employment and hoped by now one of the car plants would have called. I guess it wasn't meant to be. Mr. Sid was friendly guy and straight to the point. "I hope you have lots of patience pal, and I wish you lots of luck." "You're really going to need it going into the rental business". Now I'm thinking if this will be more of a challenge than I imagine. Time will tell. The deal is done, he shakes our hand and we're outta there! We are now real estate owners And soon to be landlords depending on how long it takes to get the place together. Who would have thought we could buy our own house and another one for income property in two years? When we came here we had nothing! God works in mysterious ways.

Story 3

Walking through the first rental house, it was hard to believe that we also owned it. We'll paint every room off white. Well, maybe a blue bathroom. I'll have to go shopping tomorrow for paint, towel racks, soap dish, tissue roller And shades. Things are going along great. I ran ad in the paper to find a tenant. I bought some rental applications at the office supply store and some one-year leases. We're Going to charge three hundred and fifty dollars a month and pay the water bill. The water bill comes out every three months so we'll see how it goes. It's the cheapest bill a person could have. The tenant will have to pay all other utilities. It's Thursday and the phone is ringing off the hook. They've been asking the basic questions, how many rooms, what kid of house is it, brick or frame and how's the neighborhood. We've got appointments to see the house at 11 a.m., 12 noon, 3 and 5 p.m. Babe started answering the phone to set up appointments for the following day just in case today's applicant's didn't work out. We've had twenty calls in two days! Everyone filled out an application and we would call him or her back regardless of our decision. Some applicants worked, some received ADC. We didn't discriminate. As long as their app met our guidelines and their income was sufficient, they could rent the house. We chose a married couple with three kids. The children were eight, five and four. The husband was a truck driver, his wife was a homemaker. The Kelly's seemed to be a nice family. A month after they moved in, a huge package was delivered at our home for them. The driver had tried to deliver it the day before and no one was home, so he didn't want to lug it back to the warehouse, so I signed for it. The package was from Tennessee. When Mrs. Kelly came home, I was outside and waved for her to come over. "I've got a package for you". She said, "Oh it must be from my ma." I had to go down south for a month cause Kelly (that's what she called her husband) had been harassing me when he would come back from one of the long haul runs. Someone told him I had been going out at night when he was away. I went to stay with my ma for a while and we made up just before we found your place. We're trying to make it work". I just stood there being very quiet and observant at the same time. I said, "Good luck and I hope everything works out." She pulled the package across the street and up the steps. Before she went in the house, she took a breather and smiled at me. I waved. "Damn"! Wait till I tell Babe we're renting to a family with big domestic problems. I hope we don't have to go through no shit with them. Is this why Mr. Sid said good luck? We've got our own problems with Babe still out of work and there are things I want to get for Marie, like a new bedroom set. I told Babe what happened when he came back from the Unemployment office. He said, "uh oh" and "you've got to be kidding". We just put it aside in our minds until two months later when one night the phone rang. It was one of the Kelly kids. "Miss Landlord, the eight year old boy would call me, "When is my mom coming home?" I said, she'd be home soon. "Are you ready for bed?" I didn't want to ask where she was. It was none of my business. "Yea, I got my pajamas on." "O.K. Is your brother and sister ready for bed too?" Yea. "Well go lay down and watch t.v. till she comes back". O.k. bye. It's 10:30. Doesn't she know she can go to jail leaving those kids like that? She must have left our number for him to call in case of an emergency, since we're just across the street. Wait till I see her. I hate to get personal with them. Things could get involved.

Somewhere down the line we might have to put them out and I wouldn't want to do that. They've got kids. I had to stop myself from thinking. "It won't go that far," I tell myself as I look toward the ceiling for reassurance. He's probably at work. I hope he doesn't get home before she does. The next day, the kids walking to school as I stood by the door. They survived the night. Marie wanted to walk to school with the other kids. I made sure they walked in groups cause there were many abandoned houses to pass and the bigger kids were such bullies. Some days I would look out the window and stare at our new investment. When summer comes, we will paint the trim on the house to brighten it up a bit. I hope they take care of while renting. I've heard horror stories about people moving in someone else's house and just tearing it apart. Then the landlord has to put lots of money back into it to get the house straightened out again to re rent. Mr. Kelly pulled up in the big rig. It had a nice sleeper cab painted bright red.

He parked on the side of the house because no big trucks were allowed on the street in front. Mr. Kelly was about Six feet, 240 pounds. The kids would run to the huge rig when he came home and jump in. Sometimes they would blow the horn and it was loud! I haven't seen her yet to ask her about the night her son called and to think about it, I probably won't. He might have gotten in trouble if her told he called me. One night while watching television, we heard a crash and the sound of glass breaking. Babe jumped up to look out and saw a man on the porch. It was Mr. Kelly. I was peeping from the side window. He ran down the steps toward his rig and started pulling Mrs. Kelly away from it. She had broken the window on the driver side and was headed to the other side when he grabbed her. "Should we call the police"? I asked Babe. Yes. No. Not yet! "He isn't hitting her or anything, she's messing that truck up though. "If she doesn't stop, he should call the police himself".

I knew it would come to this. He probably found out she was leaving the kids again. It's o.k. to go out but to leave three little ones at home alone, I don't think so. She can't find a baby-sitter or relative to watch them? The police came. I was peeping through the blinds and saw them go inside. Mrs. Kelly started talking loud and boisterous. One of the officers walked out on the porch with her and began discussing the situation. Soon Mr. Kelly and the other officer came out and went to sit in the scout car. Maybe the children were hearing too much. The cops were getting ready to pull off and I went to bed.

Story 4

A letter came in the mail today from Mr. Sid. He said a friend of his knows someone who lives on our street and the family wanted to sell their house to move into a condo. He wanted to know if we were interested. The house was selling for three grand. We had saved that much but should we invest in another house at this time? Mr. Sid gave us a number to get in touch with them and I called. We set up an appointment to look over the place. Babe and I walked down and did a once-over. It definitely needed paint and some windows needed to be replaced. Door handles were kind of shaky and loose so we know the locks had to be changed. We agreed to buy the place. That's rental number two. Thank you God. Babe hadn't been feeling well so I helped with lots of painting. I'm getting good at this! I never thought I would finish the first room. It seemed to take forever. He taught me how to do the ceiling first, then the walls. Going up the ladder to "cut" the ceiling was a little scary but I got used to being up high! Then I cut above the baseboards. Today I called the paper again to place another ad. We made appointments with six families to see the place. Once again it was time to make a decision. We chose the Langs. She was a single parent who had just separated from her husband and had a ten year old. She worked at a nursing home. When we decorated the house, all the rooms were painted antique white. Mr. Lang immediately wanted the bathroom mint green and she wanted her bathroom painted pink. I told her she could change the color if she liked but she would have to buy her own paint and do her own labor. WE installed new blinds before they moved in and she added those puffy valances. It seemed like she was into redoing lots of things pertaining to colors, even her face. That wasn't right, I know. I don't mean to talk about people but she worked on her face a lot. One day she was mildly made up and the next time you saw her she looked like a different person. Just think, when she greeted someone, they probably would think, "please don't hug me". That stuff would be all over your clothes! Their son Karl was a spoiled brat. He would whine like a baby. One day she bought him a "happy meal" home from work. When he opened it up, the toy was like one he already had. He cried and hollered about getting another one for hours. I walked over and asked "what's wrong with you Karl"? He said his mother wouldn't go back to the store to get another toy. I told him not to cry and let him know sometime they run out of a certain toy and that's probably all they had. He told me she can go to another place and get one with his lips poked out far enough for me to pop him but you know I wasn't going to hit the brat. I started cutting grass and about a half hour later I saw them leaving. It sure was hot today. This is the hottest day of the year and I should go to the park and put my feet in the water. Everyone is probably there so I'll just stay home. Marie is excited about her new brother or sister that's on the way! Yes, I decided to do it one more time before she gets too much older and before my body says, "That's all yawl". I was three months pregnant and feeling miserable in all of this heat. Most women crave pickles and ice cream. I want cantaloupe. Babe will probably turn on the fire hydrant then the whole block will be able to cool off for free. The rental business had been going along just fine, until Ms. Lang decided to buy a dog. First the dog chewed the door in the bathroom. She told us about it casually like we were going to feel sorry and offer to buy another door. "I know it's my dog and I should have bought him something to chew on but I don't have money this week to get another door". Well, I said, "it has to be taken care of so whenever you get the money that's fine with us". "It will probably be next week, ok"? Why didn't she tie the dog in the basement? Did she forget about the big backyard? I hope he doesn't chew on the baseboards of the walls because the woodwork is in perfect condition. She put "poochie" outside for a few days. As soon as it got dark, the barking started. I looked out to see if someone was lurking around and I didn't see a soul. She let him in after three hours. The next night, he barked past midnight. I didn't see her car in front of the house so I knew she was gone. I went to the window to tell him to shut up and he would stop for a couple minutes and start up again. This went on for weeks. Someone called the Humane Society And they threatened to have the police issue her a ticket if he kept it up. When I saw her in the yard, she told me what had happened and stated, "she didn't know he was making all that noise when we left him outside". Well you know now, I mumbled. They also told her if the dog was going to be outside, she would have to get a doghouse. Then the "no money" song started up again. It wasn't my problem. I was only concerned about who was going to clean up the dog shit.

Improvements done to our home by 1985

Story 5

I rolled over in bed one Sunday morning and the phone started to ring. It was Mrs. Kelly. "We got roaches over here", she said. I knew I should have let the answering machine come on. "Well they weren't in the house when you moved in so don't tell me nothing about them now". "Just go to the hardware store and get some bug spray for inside the house". Her husband should know how to use it. Then she asked, "Do we have to mix anything"? No, goodbye. I went back to sleep and Babe made the statement, "I don't know how long I can take being a landlord. Ouch, I said. Ouch what? "I think I'm going in labor". He jumped up out of bed and go this clothes on. Another one. This baby is pushing faster than Marie. Probably because I was so active helping him get the rental house together and walking all the time instead of sitting down someplace. We've been at the hospital all day. It's now 11:25 p.m. This baby tricked me and went back to sleep.

They started up again and now, I was thirsty. I told the nurse and she said, "Here, suck on some ice". She wrapped four pieces in a towel. Daddy, she called Babe, "you will have to leave". "I'm not going anywhere until the doctor comes back"! She left the room and the baby was coming. Honey go find her please. My doctor wasn't even at the hospital yet. The both of them returned to the room and they were shouting "push, push". The baby popped out just like that! "She's got her eyes open looking right at me", he said. Who needs a doctor.

Marie was happy to have a baby sister and helped me a lot. The Kelly kids would come over sometimes to check the baby out after school. I let them play on the porch since most of the time the baby would be sleeping in the afternoon. Today their mother wasn't home when they came home and they were locked out of the house. Since we had a key, I started to let them in but I don't like going in the tenants' Houses when they aren't there. What if something happened to one of the kids after they got in? It would be my fault. When she came home two hours later, she said, "you could have let them in", and I told her "no way". Having the job as a landlord, you have to be thinking twice as fast as your tenant especially when liability is an issue. I had been caught off guard today when Mrs. Lang went to the store. She asked me if I wanted anything. I was just sitting on the porch cooling off. I told her yes. Her son was riding his bike up and down the block and didn't want to go with her. I became the designated baby-sitter. She was gone an hour just around the corner! All I wanted was a bottle of Canadian water and some chips. I won't make that mistake again. You know how sometimes you just get a craving for things, well this was the time and she screwed everything up. By the time she came back, the taste was gone. Walking and talking fast she started talking about seeing her sister. "Ann was crying on my shoulder about getting an eviction notice." "I knew that was going to happen, what does she expect me to do"? Her hands were flying in the air and her voice was getting louder and louder. "Oh yea" I was thinking to myself. "I've heard this before". The desperate relative who's gong to be put out routine., Next she'll ask me and Babe is her sister can stay with them and the answer is gong to be no. Just as she said the last word, we heard a loud screech. A car almost hit Karl Jr. "I told you to watch out for cars boy"! She ran over to him and the driver got out of his car and asked if Karl was o.k. He slowly got up off of the ground and shook his leg a couple of times. She said it again, "well, you all right boy or not"? He finally responded that he was fine. I know it shook his little ass up. The driver got back in the car and drove off slowly wiping his forehead. The other kids came over and looked at his bike. Some of the reflectors h ad come off and his leg was scratched up. She started to holler at him about looking out for cars and slowing down. "You're lucky you didn't get hit by that car you brat". That was really unnecessary to call him a brat even though I knew he was. All of his friends just stood there and examined his bike like it was a piece of gold. I didn't give her a chance to talk about her sister again; it was time for me to cook dinner. "I'm going in, see you later". She started down the street with the bag she brought from the store. It sure was hot out here today!

Story 6

Do we want another house? Hell no! Another neighbor is moving. Everyone wants to go to the suburbs or on the East side of town where there are an abundance of brick homes. The homes on this street are frames and made identical to each other. I guess they don't mind the higher taxes and mortgage payments they'll be making. The current houses they live in have been paid for years ago. Later in life. I guess I'll understand the motive for their way of thinking. Babe said, "one more please"? I told him he had just fixed the toilet at the Kelly's' (a plastic toy had everything backed up) and now you want another house? The kids' blamed each other until their mother threatened to whip all of them, then the truth came out.

Mrs. Lang comes down here once a week to try to borrow something. I should have never let her borrow that pie pan. This week, she needed an egg until she went grocery shopping. Once before she wanted to use the grill to cook her ex a "barbeque dinner". What nerve. Babe kept telling me "just one more and that will be it for anymore property". I reluctantly agreed.

The Smiths' were moving next week. We paid them cash that we had saved and the amount they were asking was another blessing from God. The house was kept immaculately cause Mr. Smith was what I call a "clean sweep". His wife had gone to garage sales and accumulated a lot of items through the years. I helped him put some of the things out for bulk pickup, a once a month garbage pickup for large items. He had been sitting things out from the time he decided they were going to move. If he hadn't decided to get rid of some of the items, the house would be so cluttered. They definitely didn't have enough room to take the things with them since they were moving into an apartment at a retirement community. They had even given us some of the furniture they had.

Mr. Smith really didn't want to leave because he was born in the house seventy-five years ago. She would sweep the street when the leaves fell in the fall, she called it "getting her exercise".

They were the best neighbors you could have and we were really going to miss them. She gave us the new address and assured us we could visit them whenever we wanted and we hoped they would come back to the old neighborhood to visit us.

Marie is thirteen now and sometimes she would baby-sit for some of the neighbors. Mrs. Kelly wanted her to watch her kids for three hours one day so I said it would be o.k. She came in the house shouting "I'm not watching those kids anymore"! "They jumped on the couch and when I told them to stop, they just laughed. Somebody spilled juice and didn't clean it up". I asked her if she got paid and she was pouting, "no, she won't have it until tomorrow". Tomorrow?

"She went out with money, so you should have gotten yours"!

"What's her phone number"? I called her and she started to stutter. "Marie needs her money now", I told her. "There is something she wants to buy and I don't think she should have to wait. Will Mr. Kelly have it when he comes home"? "Oh no, I don't want her to get it from him. I'll bring the money over in a few minutes". I told her not to come over, Marie would come and get it. I slammed the phone down. This won't happen again. I had already promised myself we wouldn't get too personal with the tenants and on top of that, the kids didn't pay attention to Marie. I knew they were bad ass kids from the beginning!

Story 7

I went through the process again of putting an ad in the newspaper. There are so many people looking for a nice rental it's unbelievable. The new tenants were moving in today. They were a couple that lived with their children and wanted their own privacy instead of moving into a retirement or senior citizen housing. Their children sold the home they were living in and moved to another state. Jerold and Kathy said they had applied for Senior housing but the waiting list was extremely long. They had placed an ad in the same paper under "rentals wanted". He retired from Chrysler and she was a retired secretary at a law firm. "Just call us by our first names" he insisted when I addressed him by Mr. Hale. He said, "we old people but that Mr. and Mrs. stuff ain't necessary". He had a good sense of humor. A moving company delivered their furniture and Jerold asked Babe to connect the stove. Kathy seemed happy to be in a place of their own. "I'll have to come over sometime and tell you about the line I used to work on" he told Babe. "I put those cars together for years"! You couldn't talk to Jerold too long without him coughing all over the place. He smoked cigars and didn't care who was around and he wasn't going to put the cigar out until he got ready.

A few weeks later, I saw Kathy putting a flower garden together. The yard really looked nice. No one else in the other houses ever took time to do yard work, which I loved to do myself. All the other tenants did was cut grass, which was a requirement in maintaining their yards. Today the kids were outside enjoying every minute of the sun and someone had opened the fire hydrant to cool them off.   Jerold had just finished sweeping off his porch when one of the Kelly kids ran over to my house and said he had fallen down. I ran across the street and he was laying in an awkward position. I stared into his eyes and t hey didn't look good at all. Babe come over and started to pick him up but we let him lay there just in case something was broken and we didn't want to aggravate any injury. "Jerold", I called his name several times. "What happened to you"? "Are you o.k."? Kathy called 911. She was pretty calm considering what was happening. He was trying to move and he said "I just kind of felt tired an next thing I know I'm on my butt". "Did Kathy go to the hairdresser already", he said. No, she's in the house on the phone calling somebody and the ambulance is on the way. "I'm not getting in no ambulance, just help me up"! I told him he was staying right where he was and if they said he would be alright, he wouldn't have to get in the ambulance. Kathy came on the porch and told him to be still and shut up. That's the way she talked to him sometime. The EMT's got out of the ambulance and checked him over while he ranted and raved how he didn't want to go to a hospital. Men were like that. The only way Babe would go to a doctor was if he was bending over sick. Kathy said, "I tell Jerold he can't do a lot of things he use to do but he won't listen. "He needs to give up those cigars". The EMT's decided Jerold should go to the hospital and get checked out thoroughly and he would probably come home tomorrow. Kathy rode in the ambulance with him and I locked up the house. Kathy called me later that evening from the hospital and said the doctor believes Jerold had a heart attack. She said they would take a cab home after he's released. When they came home, Babe and I went over to the house to see how he was. "You know she ain't going to let me do nothin' and them doctors want me to stop smokin' my cigars"! "Next they'll want me to stop driving"! Then he told Kathy there was no sense in calling the kids cause they would only be worried. "I'm just fine". Kathy said she would hold off calling the kids but if he didn't stop smoking she was going to make the call.

Story 8

Today, Mrs. Kelly told me that she's pregnant again and she and her husband were trying to work on their relationship. They went to a marriage counselor and talked things over. I wonder if he knew she had been leaving the kids while he was on the road. Someone called the police on Mr. Kelley about the big rig. He had parked in front of a neighbor's house for two days and they had to park down the street. They were highly pissed. "It's your tenant", he shouted when he came down to tell Babe about the situation. "I'll talk to him," he shouted back but before the day was over, the police was on the block.

Last week the school called me about Karl Jr. Mrs. Lang wasn't home and our number is listed as the next person to call in case of an emergency. He had gotten into a fight and sat in the office two hours. I wasn't about to get up from my comfortable recliner to go get him. It wasn't my job. See, I told you. The Landlord has to refrain from getting too personal with the tenants. Last month, she called me to get a number for someone to come out and repair a screen that he had pushed out of the storm door. It cost her forty dollars. She was getting tired of the flies coming in and decided to get it fixed. Discipline, that's what it boils down to. If my kids were that bad, I would send them to a boot camp. To top it off for the past couple of months, she has been late paying rent. Babe and I went to the district court to get eviction papers, when we got back home, a note was on the mailbox. "I have the rent, stop down". I hope she has all of the rent plus twenty-five dollars late fee, plus the filing fee we had just paid to start the eviction. This shit is getting ridiculous. If she doesn't have all the money, we're going to court in two weeks and she'll have to leave the house for good. I know it's getting cold outside but she knows when it's time to pay. We have to pay our bills too. This business is our source of income. Babe warned her if it happens again, we're gong through with it. Mr. Lang still gives her money for whatever, so I don't know what her problem is. She had all of the money and said she would be on time with the rent from now on.

It's been several years now and the families weren't having any major problems (thank God) until. Mrs. Kelly called. "The basement is flooding, everything's backed up"! I called the same plumber who comes to our home whenever we have a problem. He arrived at Mrs. Kelley's and I told her if there was something taken out of the trap that belonged to her or the kids', she was paying the bill. The previous owner didn't have any problems with the plumbing so there shouldn't be any problems now. The plumber charged forty dollars just to come by and evaluate the situation and if he had to use the "snake" it would be one hundred dollars. He opened the trap in the basement and reached in, putting his arm in the hole. Two lipstick tubes came out and a plastic juice bottle.

What the hell. My eyes got so big and she looked so shocked. I left the basement and sat on the porch. Babe came down and asked what was stopping up the line. I told him about the tubes and bottle. Mrs. Kelly came outside. "I just don't know how that stuff got in there"! "Wait till the kids get home from school". I told her to "pay the man" and we left. I finally sat down to relax. The kids are in bed and Babe was watching football. Guess what happened next? The phone rings. I looked at the called I.D. and it was Jerold. It was 9:30 p.m., what could he want at this hour? He was suppose to pay his rent today but after it got dark, I figured he would wait until tomorrow. The answering machine came on and he left a message. "Hi, Its Jerold. I just wanted to pay the rent, but if you're sleep, I'll see you tomorrow". Click. Now, if I had an office, he couldn't call me any old time to say he was coming to pay rent at 9:30 in the evening. The office would be closed at 5:00. We get no respect. More troubles. Mr. Smarty pants, Karl Jr., had let the dog loose for the past couple of days. When he reconnected the chain, he did it the wrong way. During the night, the dog had gotten strangled! His mother went to feed the dog and made the shocking discovery. She was frantic and crying. He just stood there looking stupid. I walked down to the house and suggested she call the Humane Society. When they came to pick the dog up, I even had a tear in my eye.

To get my mind off of the tragedy of the day, I went to purchase a file cabinet. Landlords should keep a record of everything that's going on especially if you have to go to court of if something drastic happens in or on one of your properties. I was accumulating more and more paperwork, more that a paperclip or shoebox could handle. I was keeping receipts for tax purposes, keys and repair bills that we were responsible for. Then there were rent receipts, insurance policies and renewed leases. I had purchased batteries for everyone to put in the smoke alarms. They were a must because every week during the winter, I would read in the newspaper about kids playing with matches or houses burning down and the firefighters finding out the places didn't have smoke alarms. The City is getting stricter on Landlords about apartments and houses having smoke alarms.

Jerold and Kathy loved cats. Remember, before you rent a house or apartment, that's something else you have to consider. Do you want animals in your places? Mrs. Lang's' dog, now its Kathy's' cat. She would feed the neighborhood cats and kept one in the house without asking us. Babe and I agreed if anyone else had animals, we were charging a fifty-dollar "animal deposit". Yes, there are lots of Landlords that do it! I mentioned the cat to her because she assumed it was all right. Babe went over to repair a drip in the kitchen faucet and the cat rubbed his leg. Oh shit.

He didn't like cats. If it hadn't been for Kathy and Jerold being as nice as they are, that cat would have been history. Kathy came to the rescue and he asked her if she just had e one cat. "I bought a litter box so it wouldn't mess up anything". "Alright, as long as it doesn't mess up the walls either". "You know, they like to scratch on things". I know this is a long chapter but I have to tell you about one more scenario before I go tot chapter nine.

We were usually in bed by 11:00. One night the doorbell rang just as I laid down. Who in the hell could this be at this hour? Mrs. Lang had locked herself out of the house. This has happened two other times with another tenant. What if we didn't live on the same street? They would have to wait for someone else to come home, break a window and pay later or maybe call a locksmith! The first thing that comes out of their mouth is "I'm glad one of you were home, or, good thing you guys live close by"! To top things off, no one bothered to call us first to see if we were home, they just rang the doorbell. I did mention you have to have patience in an earlier chapter didn't I?

Big time improvements with a Master

Bedroom done by 2000.

Story 9

Our friend Charley, he was a good guy. He lived on the block for over twenty years. He always told Babe, "When I decide to leave this house, I want you to have it". Yes I know what you're thinking, but this house was an exception. Well, the time came when his health started to deteriorate. We took him to his doctors' appointments just to make sure he would get there. He had a license to drive but during a trip alone from the doctors' office, he got lost. Driving alone, he would lose his sense of direction, so we offered to make the trip with him. He complained that the doctor was giving him too much medicine so he didn't take it. He had hurt his toe and it didn't seem to heal properly. The doctor admitted him to the hospital for a week to administer to the toe and confirmed it wasn't healing. He had to be admitted to a nursing home as a resident there because there was no one to take care of him twenty-four seven at the house. That was a sad day because he had been independent for so long and we wouldn't be able to visit him everyday, not living down the street.   We had all of the paperwork done and soon we were to be owners of another rental property. Charley hadn't done any work to the house in years. It needed painting, repairs to the porch and plumbing needed to be replaced. Soon the house took on a new look and it was ready to be rented. We put an ad in the local paper again, and the calls came in. A family called the next morning to make an appointment to see the house. She was a single mother with four kids. Her name was Ms. Bell. Ms. Bell gave us a deposit on the home before I could check out her references and I reminded her if they didn't check out, we were giving her the money back. She was receiving assistance and had a part-time job. The kids like the fact there were three bedrooms. The boys would be in one bedroom, the girls in the other. They moved in two weeks later and we were happy that they were happy. She didn't have much furniture, so anything that I wasn't using I gave to them. The kids were well behaved and had manners, unlike some of the butt holes that pass by the house going to and from the nearby school. The girls were active in sports and the boys like to help Babe if he was working in the yard or cutting grass.

Oh Lord! She had a boyfriend that was married. He would come over to the house and stay a few days. Everything seemed to be going along fine until one night when the doorbell rang. It was 2 a.m.! Babe and I couldn't believe someone was at our house waking us up at that time of morning. He grabbed his "38" and went to the door. He switched on the light and asked, "Who is it"? The voice of a small child said, "Will you call the police for my mom"? What in the hell was going on? It was Ms. Bell's kids. They hadn't been in the house two months and now this! (So you want to be a Landlord, huh?) We called the police but I didn't stay awake to see if they ever answered the call. I saw the kids the next morning going to school and they seemed to be all right. We hoped the police call was no big issue and I wasn't about to get in the middle of a family dispute. Another month later, I stopped to visit and picked up the rent. She seemed to be very distant. She wasn't her friendly chatty self. I told Babe about the visit and he said maybe she wasn't feeling well. She wasn't feeling well that's for sure. Strange. She talked like she was on some kind of high and not a beer high either. She mentioned the night the kids came to the house and asked us to call the police. "I'm sorry they woke you up, it won't happen again". Just when I thought I had heard all of the stories I needed to hear about the tenants, she admitted to being on drugs in the past. She said she had a mental problem and was on medication daily. When she didn't take her medicine, she was a different person. I was thinking to myself, "I really don't want to hear all of this drama. She rattled on and on and told me her boyfriend came over that night and they started fighting. He asked her if she had taken her meds and she said no. We met him right after she moved in and he seemed like a nice guy. Then she talked about her sister. She lived with her two years, got mad at her, then took her money and kicked her out of the house. One of the kids would stay with their father, the others would stay with someone else and she was homeless until she saw the ad in the paper for our rental. This was such a sad story. I couldn't believe what I was hearing. You see cases like this on the television but you never think you would ever meet a family that was so dysfunctional. I told her I would pray for them and she was glad to hear that I understood her situation. They lived in the house for six months and she decided to move in with her grandmother who was very ill. She said if she were able, she would have bought the house from us because she liked the convenience of the stores and school.

This family had touched my heart like no other. I hope and pray today, that the children are doing fine and that their mother is getting the help and support she needs.

This is not an easy business. People that I know would say, "You've got it made". "You don't have to leave out of the house to go to a nine to five". Some of those statements would piss me off because it's not just about the money you make. You're providing a service for someone. If you purchase a "dump", it takes a lot of elbow grease and dirty hands to accomplish a livable dwelling for others. It also takes your determination and faith to endure the times of stress your tenants can place in your life when they are having a bad time. Stay prayerful. We all have issues and you should always deal with your tenants as humanly as possible. That's what makes you a successful Landlord!

In the end.

You have now read some examples of the situations that a Landlord encounters. Here are some rules to remember:

1. Get as much information as possible on the rental application.

2. Receive extra deposit money if they have a cat or dog.

3. Be courteous and polite to everyone filling out an application. They may be your next tenants.

4. Your rental units must be in tiptop shape before tenants move in. Be sure to make a videotape.

5. Have basic secretarial skills; there is a lot of paperwork and filing involved.

6. Keep a spare key handy for lockouts.

7. Do not get personally involved with a tenant. (Playing cards, having meals together, or allowing your teenager to baby-sit unless they are paid first.)

8. Get Caller ID.

— **My Personal Opinion** —

In 1986 when we purchased our first rental, it was truly a challenge. Each home was different with a personality of its' own. There would always be one more thing I wanted to do in the homes and Babe would tell me "that's enough". I am glued to the television when the home restoration shows come on. This Old House, Bob Vila to name a few. Maybe in another life, I was a Carpenter. The ideas and renovations they have on television now, we did back then. Just think, that could be me with my own show. It's not an unreachable dream. Now, in 2002, I still enjoy decorating and painting rooms in my home. I live in rural Pennsylvania and lots of homes are being built on land the Farmers have sold to developers. I stop at the sites and view them from start to finish and envision how happy the new family will be to see the finished product. When you enjoy

what you do, success if eminent!

About the Author

I am so happy that I finally finished this book!! The dream to be published started years ago but I was inspired more than ever in 1993 after the passing of my Paternal Grandmother and Favorite Uncle in the same year. I said to myself, "tomorrow is not promised, so I'd better get on the ball."

I was born in Chicago, Illinois. I wrote many poems and short stories while in school and wanted to become a teacher. God had other plans for my life.

I have two daughters, one in the Air Force, the other one pursuing a Communications Degree. Both live in Tampa, Florida. My stepson is a Sheriff in Chicago, Illinois.

My husband and I now live in Stroudsburg, Pennsylvania where we had a new home built. I am currently working on a new book with hopes of the novel to become a movie.